A Visit to TURKEY

By Charis Mather

Minneapolis, Minnesota

Credits

All images are courtesy of Shutterstock.com, unless otherwise specified. With thanks to Getty Images, Thinkstock Photo, and iStockphoto.

Cover – Thomas koch, NNER. 2–3 – Seqoya. 4–5 – 79mtk, Nerthuz. 6–7 – QQ7, a_b_t. 8–9 – LALS STOCK, Tekkol, shutterDeniz. 10–11 – Sandratsky Dmitriy, Ekaterina_Molchanova. 12–13 – TavaS, Tatiana Popova. 14–15 – Andre Chet, Nejdet Duzen, Mitzo. 16–17 – dogusoz, muratart. 18–19 – hlphoto, Esengul Alici. 20–21 – faraxshutter, Maria Studio. 22–23 – W. Bulach, Celalettin Gunes.

Library of Congress Cataloging-in-Publication Data is available at www.loc.gov or upon request from the publisher.

ISBN: 979-8-88509-976-9 (hardcover)
ISBN: 979-8-88822-155-6 (paperback)
ISBN: 979-8-88822-296-6 (ebook)

For more information, write to Bearport Publishing, 5357 Penn Avenue South, Minneapolis, MN 55419.

CONTENTS

COUNTRY TO COUNTRY

A country is an area of land marked by **borders**. The people in each country have their own rules and ways of living. They may speak different languages.

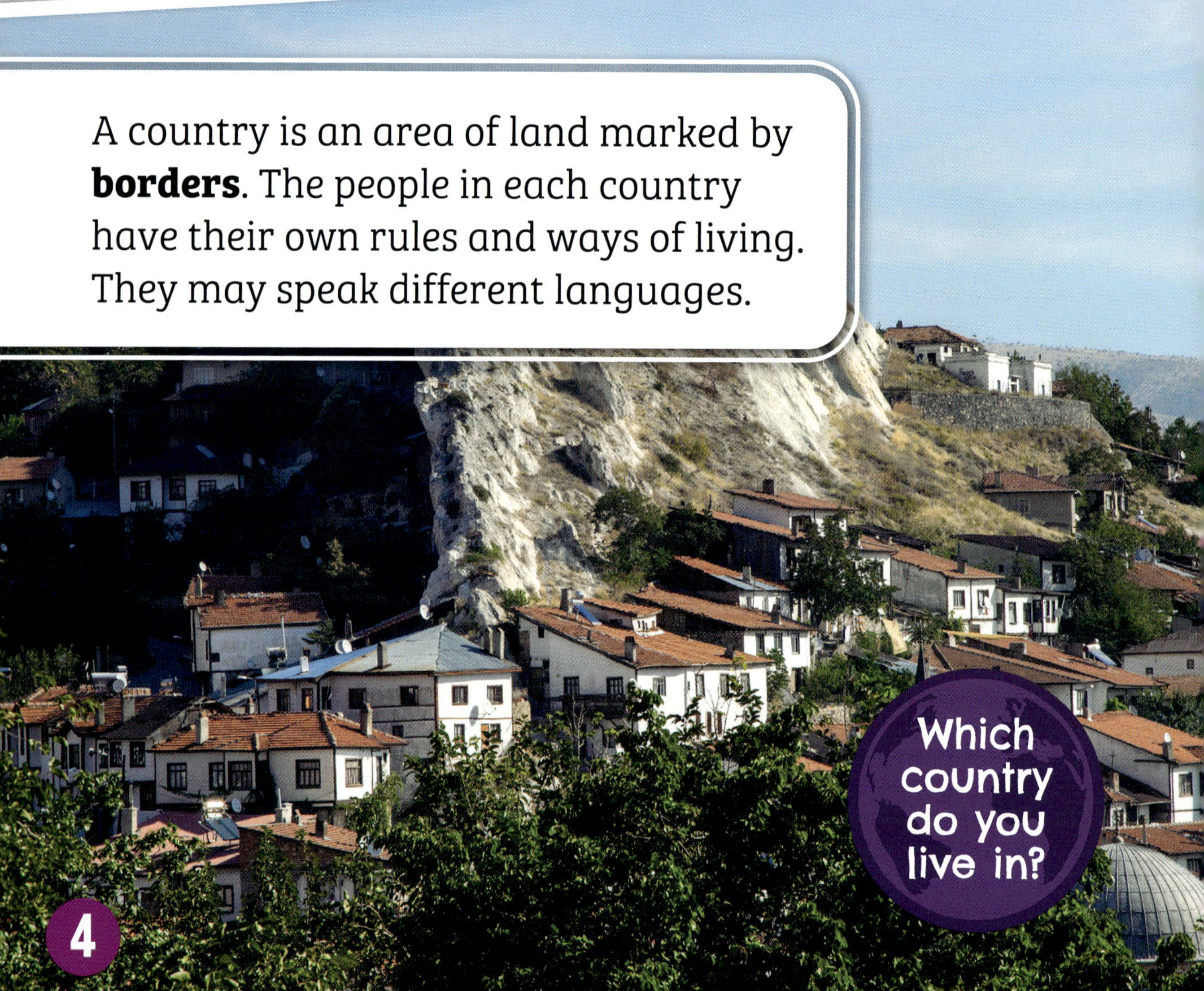

Which country do you live in?

Each country around the world has its own interesting things to see and do. Let's take a trip to visit a country and learn more!

Have you ever visited another country?

TODAY'S TRIP IS TO TURKEY!

Turkey is a country mostly in the **continent** of Asia. Part of it is in Europe, too.

FACT FILE

Capital city: Ankara
Main language: Turkish
Currency: Turkish lira
Flag:

Currency is the type of money that is used in a country.

ISTANBUL

We'll start our trip in Istanbul, the biggest city in Turkey. It is home to the Hagia Sophia, which is a famous building that was built almost 1,500 years ago.

Hagia Sophia

Istanbul has a huge covered market called the Grand Bazaar. There are about 4,000 different shops. Many sellers serve tea to people who visit their shop.

TURKISH BATHS

Turkish baths, called hammams, are very popular. They have rooms that are full of steam and are often shared by lots of people.

A visit to a hammam usually includes scrubbing with lots of bubbles. The bubbles are made by dipping a cloth bag filled with air into soapy water.

CAPPADOCIA

Next, we'll head to Cappadocia. This part of Turkey is known for its **natural** stone towers. They are sometimes called fairy chimneys. Some towers have houses cut into them.

We can take a ride in a hot-air balloon to get a good look at the fairy chimneys. Once a year, people gather here for a balloon **festival**.

PAMUKKALE

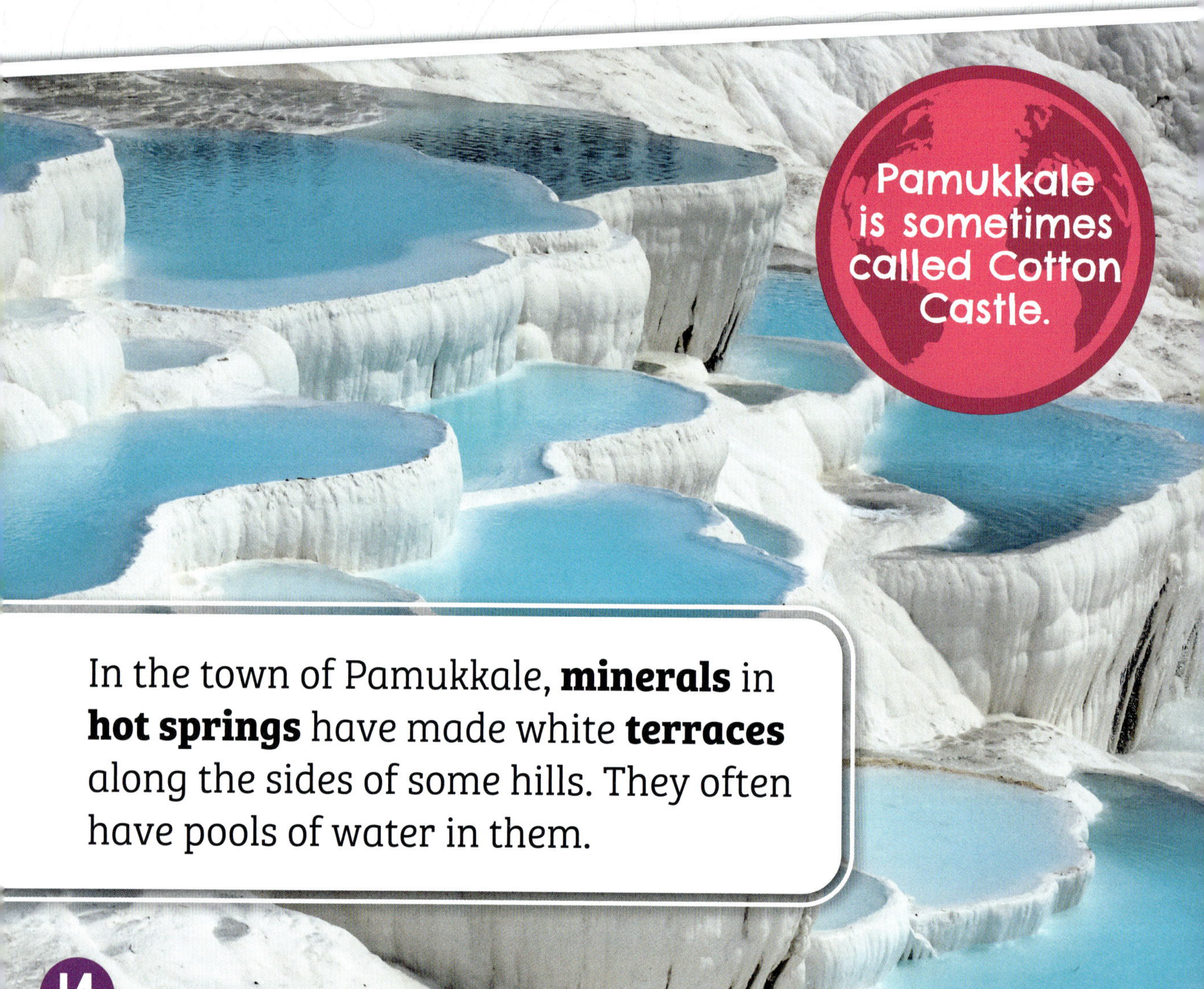

Pamukkale is sometimes called Cotton Castle.

In the town of Pamukkale, **minerals** in **hot springs** have made white **terraces** along the sides of some hills. They often have pools of water in them.

Pamukkale is also home to the **ruins** of a very old city. This city was named Hierapolis. A famous hot spring found nearby is called Cleopatra's Pool.

EPHESUS

There are even more ruins to be found in the city of Ephesus. Many people from around the world come to see what is left of its streets and buildings.

One of the most **well-preserved** ruins is the Library of Celsus. Its walls have lots of small details on them. There are even some statues.

FOOD

Feeling hungry? Let's grab some food. First, we'll try kebab. This is meat that has been cooked on a stick. Kebabs are often served with a yogurt sauce.

Baklava is a popular Turkish dessert. It is made with pieces of pistachio nuts between many thin layers of **pastry**.

DERINKUYU

Turkey has many underground cities. One is called Derinkuyu. In the past, Derinkuyu may have had about 20,000 people living in it.

Derinkuyu was made to keep people safe. The city was hidden from anybody above ground. Huge stones were used as doors.

Derinkuyu is thousands of years old.

BEFORE YOU GO

We can't forget to visit Ishak Pasha Palace. No one lives here anymore, but many people still visit and enjoy looking out over the nearby hills.

Ishak Pasha Palace

While we visit Turkish cities, we should keep an eye out for bird palaces. Some buildings have tiny, detailed palaces on their walls. These were made a long time ago for birds to live in.

A bird palace

GLOSSARY

borders lines that show where one place ends and another begins

continent one of the world's seven large land masses

festival an event where many people come together to celebrate

hot springs warm pools of water that are heated naturally within the earth

minerals substances found in nature that are not plants or animals

natural made by nature

pastry a sweet dough

ruins what is left of something made long ago

terraces raised, flat platforms of land with sloping sides

well-preserved kept in good condition

INDEX